ECLIPSE

a love story between the sun & moon

wilder
∴

also by wilder

Nocturnal
Golden
Wild Is She

Andrews McMeel
PUBLISHING®

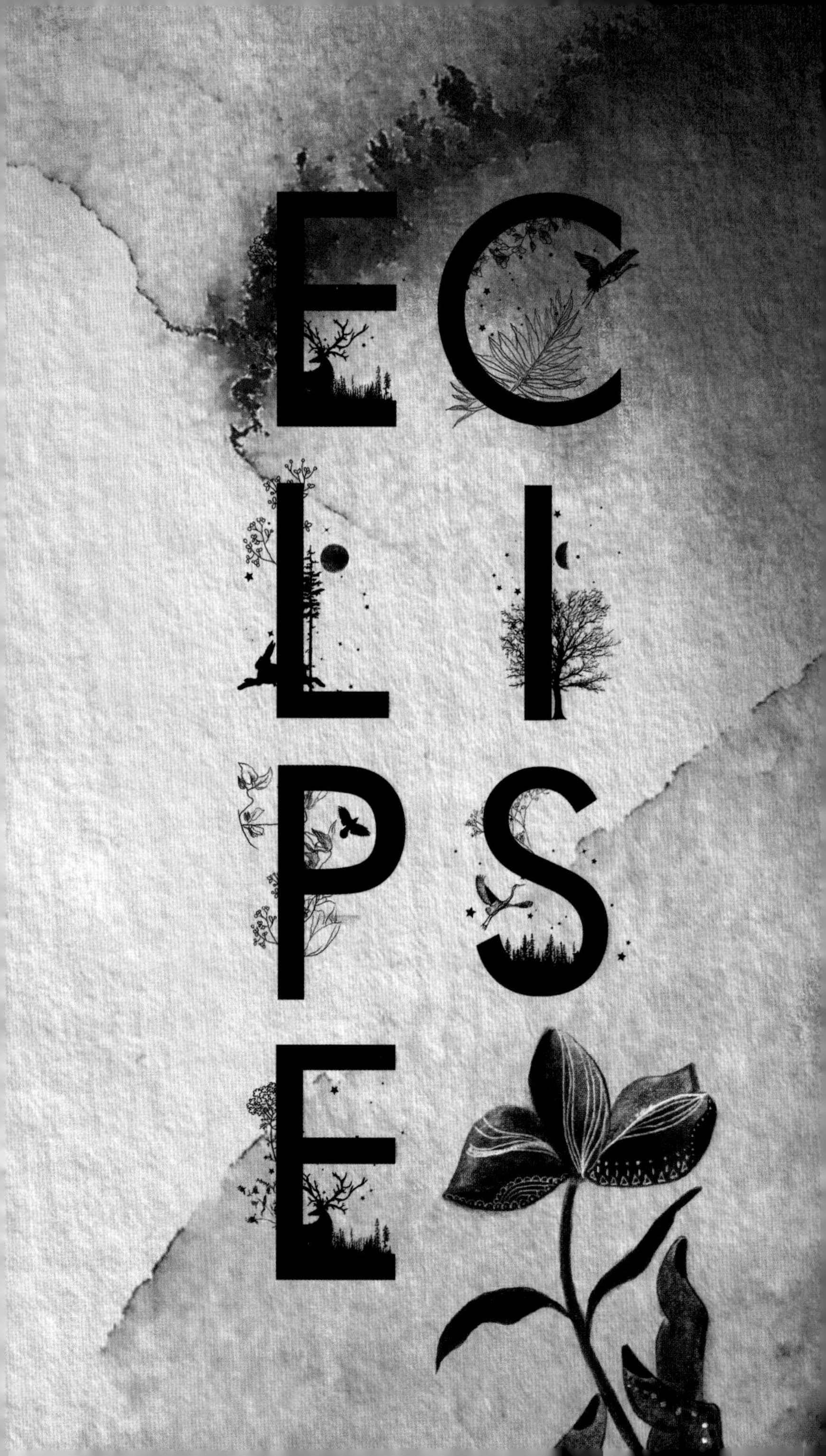
ECLIPSE

we share the kind of love they write songs
about. there is nothing more beautiful than
watching two people that keep finding each
other day after day despite all of the darkness
between them.

it's just you and me out here.
a sun & moon believing that there is hope
living among the stars and that one day
we will finally get to be together.

no one gets tired of watching
all of the ways we get to say i love you.

for jarett.

thank you for showing me
how to look at the sky

THE STARS

am i

AWAKE

or am i

DREAMING

it's a beautiful thing sharing this sky with you.

won't you stay just a little bit longer?

i live for these days when we are in the
same place at the same time.

—*the moon in the sky after sunrise*

if i don't grow,
how will i ever reach
the stars?

when i look at you i know that this is a once-
in-a-lifetime kind of love. the kind where
time stands still, but my heart still races like
it has been been running for miles. the kind
where i wake up from a good dream and i
still get to live it.

you make giving my heart away so easy
and i hope that you never want to give it back
because i've been waiting all of my life for
someone like you and i don't ever want
this story to end.

even if the lights went out
i would never stop looking for you.

even if i was blind i would know
how to find you because you never
forget the things you know by heart.

i've never known anyone else who could
make everything beautiful just by existing.

it's a delicate thing,

the way you light up every room you touch.
the way we all want to grow in your direction.
the way you make us feel better
without saying a word.
the way we can see in colour
because of the way you shine.

you're the kind of person we look at
and know everything will be okay.

you make me want to live in the moment
because i see how life can pass all of us by in
an instant and when you're standing next to
me all i want is this feeling to last forever.

so i will take my time loving you,
in this lifetime and the next,
because if i've learned anything at all
it's that you should never rush something
that you want to hold on to with all of
your heart.

the truth is,
none of us know where we will find love.
it shows up unexpectedly on a saturday
afternoon in aisle seven at the grocery store
or at the park in the middle of a summer day.

love finds us when we stop waiting for it to be
the hero of the story. it shows up when we let
go of the expectation that love from someone
else is what we need to be happy.

love will find you when you stop
looking for it in the person standing in front
of you before you've found it for yourself.

you are my perfect timing.
my smile in the dark and the reason
i feel with my whole heart.
loving you is the most effortless thing i've
ever done.

i do it when no one is watching
(and when everyone is, too).

i do it in my sleep.

i do it without trying.

i wonder if you will
find something to love
after my light lets go
just like the rest of me.

falling is the only
language we both
understand, but when
i saw hope in your eyes
as i fell from the night,
i couldn't tell if it was because
i was coming or going.

—*shooting star*

∴

the night is for
dancing under the stars
in the middle of an empty parking lot
and making a wish for all
of our dreams to come true
and believing that they will.

when the darkness starts to get heavy
and you feel like there's no end in sight,
always remember that i will carry the light
for both of us.

if i shine
then you shine, too

always remember
that on the other side of a storm
is a bright blue sky
that will find its way back to you.

have you ever noticed the way light changes
everything? the world wakes up and the birds
begin to sing while we open our eyes to a new
beginning. we wash yesterday off of our skin
and find a reason to believe that good things
are ahead of us.

you may not understand why
i look at the sky and watch the stars fall
down to earth, but i've always believed that
the act of letting go is brave.

the never knowing where you will land,
but trusting that everything will be okay.

i can't even put into words
how good it feels to see you standing over
there in the middle of all that darkness,
shining the way that you do so that
you can see us and we can see you.

there are so many things
that are unknown
in this world,
but when i saw you i knew
that i would want to smile with you
for as long as i live.

you are the kind of person the world knew
we needed.

all that beauty.
all that warmth.
all that golden light.

and how lucky am i to be in your company,
living in the same space at the same time.

the word *home* means something
different when i have you by my side.

there is this thing about you
that when anyone looks in your direction
they can't help but want to know more.
i think it's how you carry yourself—

hiding pieces of who you are one day and
showing all of you the next.

it's the kind of give and take that leaves us
wanting more.

you have our undivided attention and i don't
think we could ever get enough of you.

—*the cycle of the moon*

THE

UNIV

SHOWED ME

BEAU

IT ALL

ERSE

HOW

TIFUL

COULD BE

it's impossible not to follow your heart when
it knows there is something beautiful on the
horizon. you were waiting to be found and
i was looking in the right direction. some
might call it *luck* but i call it *meant to be*
because of all the stars that live in this sky,
you were the only one that caught my eye.

my heart knew you before the rest of me did
and for the first time in my life, i'm not afraid
of falling.

when you shine all your light
in my direction
i can finally stop hiding
and show all of me.
i can finally be who i've
always wanted.

—*full moon*

when you start to wonder
if you are enough,
always remember that
you grow gardens
without even trying.

you are so loved
all of the flowers
want to grow toward
you.

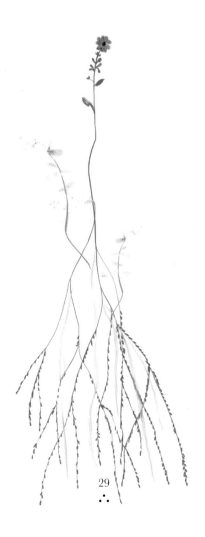

they look up to us for answers
making wishes as we fall to earth,
but what they don't know is that it's them
who make all of our dreams come true.

—*stars & humans*

we look at the world and it looks back at us
with eyes that believe anything is possible
because we exist. we are the main characters
in their memories—

a sunset by the ocean,
a full moon in the mountains.
a sun and moon that show up
at the same time.

isn't it amazing,
having so much love to give?
they can't help but notice
that when we have each other
we have everything we need
and they do, too.

i talk to the stars about you.

i do, too.

i never thought i would meet someone
who loves talking about the stars
as much as i do.

*no one understands forever
like you and me.*

every day the view is different,
but that doesn't mean it changes
the way i look at you.

you are what daydreams are made of
and that's all i could ever want.

you have glitter in your hair and your heart is the colour of gold. it's so full and honest like the wildflowers on the side of the road that can't help but look in your direction . . . just like me.

so let's keep dancing in circles and see where it takes us. i'll be the mirrorball that reflects all of your light. little pieces of brilliance that fill the sky with everything any of us could need.

for now.
for always.
forever.

when you rise
i do, too.
i can't help but follow you
wherever you go.

i hope you never forget
these moments when it all feels perfect.
when there's nothing that can stop
us from being two people who
are so in love that everything else
falls into place.

i'll keep wearing my heart on my sleeve
if you promise to keep carrying hope in your
pockets because sooner or later i know
we will be able to get this right.

when i look at you

everything is

GOLDEN

without even trying you taught me how to
look at the dark and not fear it, but mostly
you showed me that it's possible to love
myself and feel something so extraordinarily
beautiful for someone else at the same time.

there's enough love to go around
for both of us

but do you even understand
how dark, cold, and lifeless this world
would be if you weren't here?

of all the stars
i've ever known
the most beautiful
i've met
is you.

because of you,
our eyes know colours that we
didn't even know could exist.

you make our life
a little more beautiful
every day.

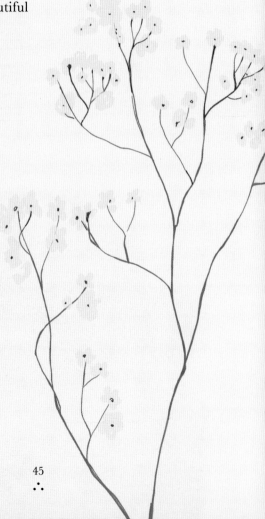

i hope our story never has an ending
that my heart wants to change.

p.s.

it's so lonely when you're gone and even
though i know you'll always come back, i still
wait for you wondering how i would survive
if you didn't.

for some it may be a graveyard of stars,
but for others it's a sky full of dreams
that have yet to come true.

perspective is everything

if you give me enough time,
i'll show you everything that i've ever
loved about the way you are.
starting from your smile down to the way
you make the worst day feel like a dream
come true.

i hope you never become a stranger
because i've gotten used to having you
around. i'm not even sure forever would be
long enough for all this love i have left to
give.

∴

open your eyes.

i want you to see

the dream come true.

BETWEEN

it hurts,
knowing that you can never be touched
by the thing you love the most.
i see the way you look at me,
the way you face my direction
and shine like my light is all that you
have ever wanted.

you seem so close,
but you are always too far away.
spinning. dizzy.
and during those moments when
you hide behind the world
all i can do is stand still
and wait for you to find your way
back to me.

—*the sun waiting for the moon*

*i hope no one ever
has to miss anything
this much.*

and what a gift it is
that you are the closest star
in my sky.

the way we shine
is a reflection of all that you give.

i hope you remember to save some of that
light for yourself.

isn't it amazing that we get to keep
finding each other day after day
knowing that this will be our view
for the rest of our lives?

and in those moments when i show you my
darker side, just know that i will find my way
back to you.

you are the home i will always come back to

there will be days you wake up feeling small,
like the world is against you, but
everything that is beautiful looks small
from a distance.

they do not need to ask me why i love you
because it was love at first sight for all of us.
we admire you from a distance knowing that
no matter what happens, you will be here
through every season,
the good and the bad,
and we will never have to wonder
if you will come back tomorrow.

you fill me up
and i am floating.

loving you is like a
sunday morning in bed all day
kind of love,
an *everything will be okay*
kind of love,
an *i'm not hungry because i'm so full of you*
kind of love.

thank you for helping me
believe in better days when i couldn't see
them myself.

thank you for loving me back even though
it feels like the world is trying to keep
us apart.

you make my heart feel like
a summer day in june.
there is so much to look forward to now.
the days are getting longer and
everything is coming back to life.

and when you pulled me out of the darkness
you reminded me that there's always
something worth waking up for
in the morning.

my eyes are finally open and this view
is too beautiful to miss.

sometimes it feels like it's just
you and me in this universe
fighting for a chance to have our
happily ever after, but even if
i have to love you from a distance
for the rest of my life, i will spend every day
showing you that we are worth the wait.

and isn't it

magic

the way the universe
introduced me to you

people look up to you because you give them
something to look forward to. so don't spend
your time believing that you're not enough,
because i promise, you are so much more
than that.

when they say nothing good can last forever,
i look at you and know that isn't true.

and what an honor it has been
having a front row seat to every season of
your life.

and what a gift it has been to be able to share
all of my phases with you knowing that we
will keep showing up for each other through
all of the changes.

it's a heavy feeling
knowing that everything as we know it
might stop if we don't keep going.
sometimes i just want to stand still and take
some time for myself and not feel like the
weight of the world is on my shoulders,
but when i look at what's around me
i am reminded that we all survive
because of balance.

so take a deep breath and remember to be
gentle with yourself because the things you
take care of will take care of you, too.

and what we have to hold
is a glimmer of hope that's out there
in the distance.

the stars keep shining down on all of us
so that our dreams stay alive
and our hearts do, too.

if ever there is as moment you think that
maybe you feel too much,
just remember that there is a
whole universe living inside of you.

the truth is,
i've been dreaming of you since the very
beginning. it was in the way you blinded
me with all that light. i lost sight of who i
was and became a better version of myself
because you showed me that change wasn't
something to run away from.

sometimes i don't know whether i'm coming
or going, but what i know for sure is that i am
exactly where i'm meant to be.

right here.
standing across from you.
the most beautiful show on earth.

imagine being so powerful
that the whole universe stays silent.

you are the greatest love i've ever known.
the way you give out your light
on days when we have forgotten
how to create our own.

i hope someday you're able to see yourself
the way that we do. we can't help but stare
at your beauty day after day. and when you
leave, we count down the days until you come
back again because none of us can imagine
life without you. your presence gives us
something to believe in when everything feels
dark and empty.

don't you see how amazing you are?
even the oceans move because you
ask them to.

that's the thing about me. i've never been
able to do anything quietly. i love with my
whole heart and give every part of myself
away so that others can feel better.

we all deserve to feel like sunshine
on a cloudy day.

i live for rainy days
and the way it reflects my light,
creating colours in the sky,
giving everyone a reason to smile
even though the skies are grey.

YOU

MAKE

THE MOST

BEAUTIFUL

SUNSETS

i will keep showing up
again and again
to remind you that even if yesterday
was not a good day, tomorrow has the
potential to be something beautiful.

give yourself another try

there are going to be days
that will make you feel like giving up
before trying. it's okay to move slow and take
a step back for a little while until you're ready
to keep walking again.

what you should know is,
you still have so much room to grow
and when you do, you will find yourself
looking in different directions
along the way.
if you don't like the view,
change the way you're facing.

the sun doesn't stay in one place
and you don't need to either.

you deserve someone
who wants to take the time
to get to know you by heart.

i think it's beautiful the way
i can see right through you.
you say, maybe it's because i'm empty,
but don't you know it's your clarity
that allows my light to get in?
they say good things come
in threes, and i know it must be true
because together we fill the sky
with an endless circle of color.
even though it's just for a moment,
at least we gave their eyes something to see.

i always knew i would find the words
i love you hidden in grey skies
with a chance of rain.

—*things the sun tells the rain*

on days you feel like change is taking longer
than you think it should, trust the process and
know that everything will fall into place when
the timing is right.

it takes the sun 365 days to walk around the
earth. it's okay if it takes a while to get where
you want to be.

there are storms that let go when the pressure
becomes too much and no one looks at the
sky and asks it why.

let your feelings be honest

when you think of me
i hope that you see a future where i get to
wake up to you every morning and fall asleep
holding your hand. i hope you never get tired
of looking on the bright side because i
promise i will always love the darker side of
you that you fear will make me want to leave.

when i open my eyes all i can see is forever
and from where i'm standing the view looks
pretty good from here.

even though there is all this space between us,
i'll always be here fighting for our love story
because i will keep waiting for as long as it
takes.

are you okay?

*i think i just need
some of your light.*

i've been meaning to tell you
that we have a lot to look forward to.
so many stars to kiss goodbye,
so many wishes to make,
so many dreams to come true.

i spend my nights
connecting the dots
between you and me,
waiting for the day
when they will lead
me straight to you.

i can't wait to hold you
when all this waiting is over

i wake up with you on my mind
and see you in my dreams when i'm asleep.
you are everywhere to me, but you're still not
within reach.

i hate being far from you.

i wish the stars would give us a turn and
make just one of our dreams come true.

ever since the first time i saw you
shining in the corner of the room,
i couldn't help but see something
so honest, so warm, so full of
all the things that make a person
feel good inside.

i knew that i wanted to walk
beside you for as long as
you would let me.

*i'm so glad i found what was
missing from me*

i think i'll take the long way home
if it means i get to spend
a little more time with you.

my favorite part of the story was when
you were ready to show me everything you
used to hide.

i gave you all of me
and you gave me all of you

this is me
trying to hold myself together—
begging time to stand still
(just for a little while)
because i don't know
if i can say goodbye to
another day like this.

but when you turn toward me
i am reminded how much
~~light~~ love we have left to give.
so today i will live in the moment
knowing that even when
you start to look the other way,
we will find each other
again and again.

and every lifetime with you

will always be the best one

i will never forget
the night i found you in halves.
you told me you felt like
something was missing,
but i knew with a little
bit of time and light
you would be full again.
i think it's beautiful
the way you
disappear in pieces—
the way you
hide parts of yourself
away for a while
until you're ready
for us to find you.

and when you say to me
maybe i'm broken,
i think to myself,
maybe you are.
but it's okay. we all go
through phases.
we are all surviving
something.

YOU & ME

we are so
alone out here.

that's all i've ever wanted.

this is us
holding the universe together
like a pinky holds a promise.
even though i am broken in halves,
i know you will always find me.

—*quarter moon*

i hold time between my hands
hoping it will stand still
long enough for you to find me.
and when you said i was
the colour of your favorite dream,
i knew you could see what
i was made of—
even if it's true that
what goes up must come down,
i will fall with you under a sky
that leaves us closer than
where we started.

i do not have a dark side.
these are just the places where i miss
the sun the most.

—*new moon*

i think i'll always feel
like you are missing
from me.

i just want to hold hands
and let the time pass by
like there's nowhere else
we need to be.

without even realizing it,
you changed the way i look at the sky.
i no longer fear what i can't control and
you showed me how to find beauty
in everything.

you're the reason there is hope waiting for me
on the other side of darkness.
i can feel the light getting closer and i'm
starting to see how different it can be with a
little bit of patience and a whole lot of hope.

you believed in me
when i didn't believe in myself

it's okay if you lose yourself in the
dark for a little while, but please don't take all
that love with you when you leave.

you are known for so many
beautiful things,
but the way you light up the world
(in my eyes)
will always be your greatest
gift.

you are the kind of magic i can't take my eyes
off of. the way you disappear so quietly and
come back like you never left,
with iridescent skin that lights up the night in
the most effortless ways.

you are a masterpiece
i could admire forever.

call it what you want,
but i think we are a story meant
for the movies. a love like this deserves
to be the center of attention. they look at us
while we keep dancing to our own music,
shining light back and forth across the sky
living like the world might end tomorrow,
but knowing the both of us will keep
living forever and ever.

you are the
good days
i look forward to
when life starts
to feel heavy.

i live for the nights when you come back after
being away. even though you tell me that
you'll see me again soon, i still catch myself
holding my breath . . . waiting . . . standing on
my tiptoes because time doesn't move fast
enough when i am missing from you.

and isn't it amazing . . .
i didn't even need to wait to find you?
it was love at first sight and we haven't
stopped looking at each other
ever since.

don't you see how beautiful you are?
when you look at me, what you see is a
reflection of you. i am shining all of this light
back in your direction, not because i think
you need it, but because i want you to
understand just how breathtaking
it is to see the way you make everything
so much better.

we keep waiting for something to change, but
there you are, millions of miles away,
and here i am, desperately trying to find a
way to be closer to you.

at least we live
in the same universe

the stars know you the same way i do
because i can't get you out of my head and
speaking your name is one of the ways
that makes it feel like you are close to me.
i make wishes into the dark just like
everyone else because if i don't have hope,
what do i have left besides a heart on the
verge of breaking from missing you too
much.

sometimes i wonder if you talk
to the stars about the way you miss me, too.

i just wanted you to know
that i will still be here
admiring you
even in those moments
when you look away.

i will keep finding you
even when it's dark

you are the reason people write poetry.

everything about you is a poem. the way you
bring things back to life after being buried
under the winter's snow. the way you make a
day worth waking up for. the way you turn
the things you touch to gold and we can't
help but smile because it just makes
everything beautiful. the way you take your
time to get to where you want to be. slow and
steady on your feet no matter what is thrown
your way. we all look at you and understand
your beauty. accepting you just the way you
are and never wanting you to be different.

i close my eyes knowing that
the bad dreams will never find me
when i have you to wake up to.

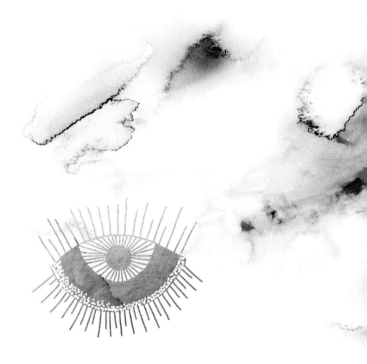

you make my heart feel better
in moments when it's hard to love myself.
i have a hard time putting it into words, but
what i'm trying to say is that every
part of my day has felt lighter ever since i
saw you standing there across the room.
from the first time my eyes saw you
i knew there was something that was meant
to be. everything started to make sense
and i stopped worrying about the things i
couldn't control because even though i felt
like i was losing my mind, i knew it was
because it was making its way to you.

you are my safe space.
my light in the dark.
my everything.

why do you love the moon?

*because it always comes
back around.*

the more you hide
the more i want to get to know you.
there is nothing about who you are
i couldn't fall in love with,
so please don't be afraid
to show me everything
that you're made of because
i am not afraid of your dark.

maybe in another galaxy
you and i will meet again
and this time you won't be
so far away.

the way i love you is out of control
in the most beautiful way.
sometimes it feels like the room is spinning
nonstop and i'm starting to understand what
it means when people say they are *head over*
heals for someone, because i still can't tell if i
am right side up or upside down.

this is the kind of love you wait your whole
life to find. the kind where others look at you
and know that it's meant to be and they hope
one day others will look at them and think
the same.

you looked me in the eyes a little longer
than i expected and i smiled from the inside.

that feeling never left me.

just in case you ever wonder
if things are different.

they are . . .

today i love you more.

no matter how dark
i get, i can promise you
that i will always carry
your light with me
and love you with all
that i am and all that i have
yet to be.

i'm the kind of person
who likes to be alone,
but it's so much better
being alone with you.

i am the dreamer

and you are

my dream.

i am terrible at playing games,
but i have mastered the art of hide and seek.
no matter how many seconds pass us by
i always find myself behind you twice in a
day. just when i start to wonder if it's too
much, i hear you say,

isn't it beautiful that i get to be the last thing you
touch before every hello and after each goodbye.

it was then i realized,
i have never really wanted to hide
i've just wanted to know i was found.

—*a rising and setting sun*

the timing of our love story
will always be the most beautiful
thing that has ever happened to me.

*i'm not
broken,
i'm just trying
to be
whole*

i don't think you realize how much
you inspire us to keep going . . .

it takes courage to keep shining
the way that you do.

the view looks pretty good from here.
every star feels like it belongs to us,
like a fireworks show that keeps going.
like a party that's never over because
the universe knows we have a
love worth celebrating.

we are a grand finale
worth staying up for.
we light up the sky so effortlessly
and when they look up at us,
they think we are some kind of magic
and the most beautiful part about that
is they are right.

you are my favorite reason
to lose sleep.

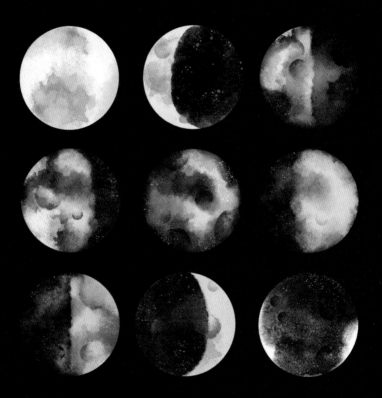

i may not be very good at finding the right
words to say, but even if i could, there are not
enough that would ever be able to express
how stunning you are to me. to witness you is
to be surrounded by a field of wildflowers. i
hold you in between my hands, blow you out
into the wind, and make wishes that i hope
will come true. i'll never grow tired of this
point of view. so vibrant . . . so breathtaking.

and i think it's beautiful the way you keep
coming back. growing in the places we never
thought love could. showing our eyes that
there is still so much more left to see.

every day is an adventure
when i spend it with you.

when you move
i move too

one of the things i love most about who you
are is that i can tell you how i feel and not
wonder if you are listening.

i hope when you think of me
you remember the good days and all of the
memories we have made along the way.
i hope when you think of us you feel like
sunshine from the inside out because you
deserve a garden at your feet no matter
the season.

all i could ever want is to be the reason you
have a million different reasons to smile
because i've been living with one on my face
for an eternity and this feeling is too good not
to share.

and it all started with a single moment—
nothing but you, me, and the night sky.

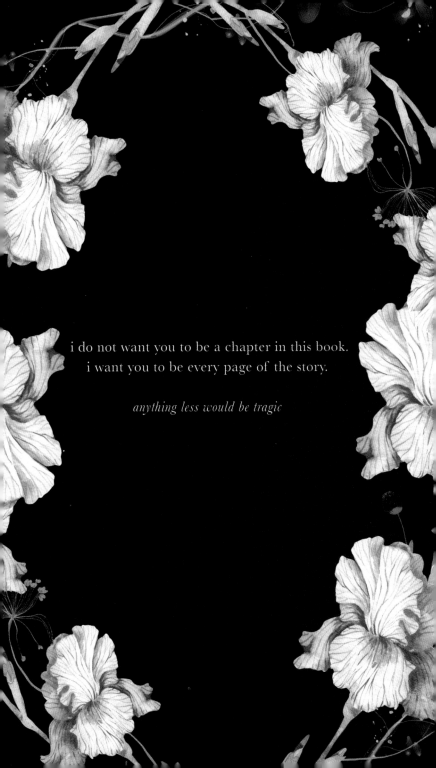

i do not want you to be a chapter in this book.
i want you to be every page of the story.

anything less would be tragic

please wait just a little while longer.

wherever you are,
i'll be there soon.

don't worry,
i'll always be waiting
right where you left me.

when they see us from earth
we look closer than we will ever be.

that's enough for me to keep trying.

this isn't the end

this is only the beginning

WITH GRATITUDE

to jarett, my favorite star in the sky. i will
never run out of ways to love you. i will never
run out of ways to tell you.

to mom, dad, larry, and family, without you i
would never know how to reach for the sky.

to jess, thank you for always being such a
bright light in the dark.

to sam, my path is so beautiful because you
are by my side.

to james and courtney, thank you for helping
me keep all of my dreams alive.

to the andrews mcmeel family, thank you for
giving my dreams a place to land.

to you, thank you for keeping these words
close. if you are home, then i am, too.

Andrews McMeel Publishing
a division of Andrews McMeel Universal
1130 Walnut Street, Kansas City, Missouri 64106

www.andrewsmcmeel.com

24 25 26 27 28 TEN 10 9 8 7 6 5 4 3 2 1

ISBN: 978-1-5248-7580-0

Library of Congress Control Number: 2023940274

Editor: Patty Rice
Designer: wilder
Production Editor: David Shaw
Production Manager: Shona Burns

ATTENTION: SCHOOLS AND BUSINESSES
Andrews McMeel books are available at quantity
discounts with bulk purchase for educational,
business, or sales promotional use. For information,
please e-mail the Andrews McMeel Publishing
Special Sales Department:
sales@amuniversal.com

wilderpoetry.com

follow the visual story on instagram:
wilderpoetry